I0800815

IMAGES
of America

WEATHERFORD HISTORIC WALKING TOURS

The Sam Lanham Chapter of the United Daughters of the Confederacy erected this Confederate monument on Courthouse Square, beginning with its base in 1915. The statue was placed on the base on November 25, 1925. It is a replica of a Confederate monument in Chickamauga & Chattanooga National Military Park in Tennessee. (Trina Haynes.)

ON THE COVER: Students gather on the grounds of Weatherford College. (Courtesy of WPL.)

IMAGES
of America

WEATHERFORD HISTORIC WALKING TOURS

Trina M. Haynes

ARCADIA
PUBLISHING

ISBN 978-1-4671-3011-0

Published by Arcadia Publishing
Charleston, South Carolina

Printed in the United States of America

Library of Congress Control Number: 2013939209

For all general information, please contact Arcadia Publishing:
Telephone 843-853-2070
Fax 843-853-0044
E-mail sales@arcadiapublishing.com
For customer service and orders:
Toll-Free 1-888-313-2665

Visit us on the Internet at www.arcadiapublishing.com

This book is dedicated to Oatis Haynes, for encouraging me to take my love of history and this town and bring to life charming Weatherford.

Contents

ACKNOWLEDGMENTS

My father-in-law, Oatis Haynes, was the first person to help me get started putting this book together. With that spark, I started making contacts and piecing together historical facts about places in Weatherford.

Kathleen Baker, the retired president of the Parker County Historical Society, spent many hours on the phone with me discussing all the great history this town had to offer. I also met with V.A. Littleton, the granddaughter of Alex Rawlins, of Rawlins Monuments, through her son-in-law Dave Deison. She had numerous photographs of her grandfather's business, and meeting with her was really taking a step back in time.

Bob Glenn, the executive vice president of PlainsCapital Bank, grew up in Weatherford and owns the Franco Texas Land Company building, which was the office of Gov. Samuel Willis Tucker Lanham at one time. Glenn had some restoration done to the building, but kept a door frame, just to keep a little bit of history. His father was a police officer and also worked in the old city hall building.

One of my most treasured meetings was with Mary Kemp, of the Kemp-Shaw family, and her very dear friend Leon Tanner. Kemp offered me details about the Kemp-Shaw Ranch, how she helped Weatherford obtain 17 historical markers, and about her efforts as part of the Abandoned Cemetery Association to memorialize sites that were no longer visible to everybody. Tanner, with whom she grew up, shared tales of their days of watermelon seeding.

Christy Bellah, the cataloguing librarian for the Preserving and Enhancing Access to Culture and History (PEACH) project at the Weatherford Public Library, helped me go through the archives for photographs. She always had something to share with me, and I appreciate her love of history and her taking the time to help with the process of accessing photographs for this book. I am also very thankful for her assistant, Amberley Parker, the PEACH digitization clerk at the library, for letting me invade her office on numerous occasions.

And I thank all the staff at Weatherford Public Library (WPL) for their help with my research, especially Martha Tandy, for her time and effort. I encourage readers to donate photographs, documents, and any type of memorabilia to the PEACH project of the Parker County Library Association.

INTRODUCTION

In the 1840s, when settlers started to arrive and make this location their home, Indian raids were a constant battle, and pioneers had to build their homes to protect themselves from such attacks. In 1855, Parker County was created by the Texas state legislature and named for pioneer and state representative Isaac Parker. Weatherford, incorporated in 1858, was named for the state senator for this district, Thomas Jefferson Weatherford (1811–1867), of Dallas. According to a descendant of Senator Weatherford's, he never set foot in his namesake town.

In 1854, the Thomas Jefferson Shaw family moved to Parker County and settled in Nebo Valley, which was later called Shaw Creek. This was extreme frontier land at the time, as there was not another settlement nearby. Five miles to the west, however, a band of Tonkawa Indians was camped on the Brazos River. Shaw built his first log cabin near what is now Highway 51; it was later moved to Log Cabin Village in Fort Worth. He built his second log cabin in 1856 on the north side of Nebo Mountain. This was their family home until his death in 1904. Thomas Jefferson Shaw signed a petition to help Parker County become established, and Isaac Parker then carried it by horseback to Austin. On December 15, 1855, Parker County was established. The 400 acres of land that the Shaw cabin sits on were purchased by the V. Kemp Jr. family in 1972. The Kemp-Shaw family opens the cabin for tours every year.

In 1866, cattle driver Charles Goodnight invented the first chuck wagon, which catered to cowboys on cattle drives along the Goodnight-Loving Trail, which was named for him and Oliver Loving and inspired the book and television miniseries *Lonesome Dove*. With Loving and Bose Ikard, Goodnight drove the first cattle across the trail. Oliver Loving was killed after an Indian attack a year later, and Goodnight drove his body by wagon back into Weatherford, where he was laid to rest in Greenwood Cemetery. Ikard, a freed slave, was recalled by Charles Goodnight as a hardworking and honorable friend.

Samuel Willis Tucker Lanham and his wife, Sarah Meng, moved to Weatherford in 1868, where he taught school in one room of a log cabin and lived in the other room. At the same time, he studied law and was admitted to the bar in Weatherford in 1869. He was appointed district attorney for the 13th district of Texas by Gov. Edmund J. Davis in 1871 and served through 1876. In July 1871, he prosecuted Kiowa Indian chiefs Santana and Big Tree for their part in the Warren Wagon train raid. Lanham went on to serve in the US House of Representatives and as the 22nd governor of Texas. Other successful local attorneys included R.B. Hood, who began his practice in Weatherford in 1893 and served for four years as the county attorney. Hood's assistant, Preston Martin, went on to engage in many legal battles with Hood in the courthouse, but they remained close friends.

The railroad reached Weatherford at 12:00 p.m. on May 27, 1880, and the first train arrived one week later, on June 4. Weatherford immediately became a shipping point for Parker County farmers and ranchers.

In 1880, David S. Switzer became the head of Granbury High School. He transformed the school into a college and led it to establish a reputation for high academic standards. In 1889, Granbury College moved to Weatherford and combined with Grover Cleveland College to form Weatherford College. Switzer continued as the president of the school. With the assistance of his wife, Rebecca (Mays) Switzer, a music teacher whom he married in 1873, Switzer offered a variety of liberal arts courses. He resigned the presidency in 1902 to open his own school, Switzer Women's College, in Itasca.

In 1891, J.D. Baker moved to Weatherford from Dallas and soon established the Baker-Poston Company. He was involved in many business ventures, including the wholesale grocery firm of Cameron, Hill & Baker, of which he was a member; the First National Bank, of which he was president; and Crystal Palace Flouring Mills Co., of which he was the director. He was also largely instrumental in the establishment of Weatherford College, and his loyal support was most helpful in the advancement of the school in its early years.

In 1913, a star was born in Weatherford: Mary Martin, who became a famous Broadway personality especially known for portraying Peter Pan. Her son Larry Hagman also became a very popular star on the hit television series *Dallas*. Our hearts were saddened to hear of Hagman's passing on November 23, 2012.

British portraitist Douglas Chandor married Weatherford native Ina Kuteman Hill in 1934. They returned to Weatherford, where they lived in her family's mansion. For the rest of his career, Chandor spent half of each year in New York and the remaining time in Weatherford, where he developed the grounds of his estate into a showplace they named White Shadows Gardens. He and Ina worked tirelessly in the gardens until his death in 1953. Ina renamed their masterpiece Chandor Gardens as a tribute to her husband.

One

Courthouse Square

Weatherford has had four courthouses. The first was completed in 1856 and had only one room. The second, built in 1858, was destroyed by fire on May 13, 1874, along with most of the early county records. The third courthouse, built in 1880, was destroyed by fire in 1884. The fourth, the current Parker County Courthouse, seen here, was completed in 1886. In 1956, restorations began on the building, with a new roof and a new face on the clock added. (Courtesy of Jeff Hicks.)

This drawing shows the first courthouse. The 18-foot-by-30-foot one-room building was constructed of rough pine lumber hauled in by ox teams. The building was completed in time for the court session beginning on November 13, 1856. (Courtesy of Mary Kemp.)

This artist's drawing was created from descriptions of the second courthouse. The two-story building was constructed of bricks manufactured in Weatherford. On May 13, 1874, it was destroyed by fire along with most of the county records. (Courtesy of Mary Kemp.)

The photograph above, taken in 1936, shows the location where the first district court of Parker County was held. It was held north of Weatherford in Parker County until the first courthouse in Weatherford was built. The historical landmark underneath the tree is the only marker of the event. The marker is seen up close below. (Both courtesy of Mary Kemp.)

Courthouse Square was always a gathering place for farmers to sell produce and hold events. Farmers would sell their newly baled cotton from their wagons in the square, which was also the sight of a few hangings in the late 1800s and early 1900s. This photograph, dated October 2, 1908, shows a car show or perhaps a race.

This crowd is gathered on the square to witness a hanging. The last legal hanging, which is believed to be only the second legal hanging, took place in May 1907 after the murder conviction of J.B. Cason in southwest Weatherford. (Courtesy of WPL.)

In 1874, R.W. Kindel began his drug business, which was so successful that he had to extend it to wholesaling as well. In 1886, he founded the area's first castor oil mill, which still stands on Front Street. (Courtesy of WPL.)

Carter Callaway's dry goods store carried the basic mercantile products of the time. Seen here around 1930, the building still stands today. (Courtesy of WPL.)

The photograph above shows watermelons being sold on the square in 1913. Preston Martin's law firm is on the far right. The father of Mary Martin, his law firm was in the Cotton-Bratton building, which still stands today. Wagonloads of watermelons were sold locally, and some were shipped as far as New York. Below, local melons were placed on exhibit at the 1904 Louisiana Purchase Exposition in St. Louis. All other melon exhibits at the world's fair were insignificant compared to the Parker County melons. Some of them had to be cut open for disbelieving spectators. Since that time, Parker County melons have been famous and in demand. (Both courtesy of Mary Kemp.)

The three-story, brick First National Bank, on the corner of Fort Worth Street, opened for business on July 1, 1880, organized by Sam Milliken. It has the oldest national charter in Texas and is the fifth-oldest national bank in Texas. It later joined the Merchants & Farmers Bank in remodeling, updating to a more modern look. (Courtesy of WPL.)

Citizens National Bank was established in 1868 by Tennessee native James Robertson Couts. In 1871, the bank was originally known as Hughes, Couts & Company, and the name changed one more time before J.R. Couts was granted a federal banking charter, which was filed under Citizens National Bank. In 1885, a two-story, stone building was completed on the corner of the square. The bank has remained in the same location for over 100 years, and a historical marker sits outside. (Courtesy of Weatherford College.)

The Carson & Lewis Hotel, seen here in the 1890s, was a prominent, two-story Weatherford hotel. It was considered a landmark on the west side of the square for many years. It was convenient to the post office and the rest of the business center. (Courtesy of WPL.)

In 1883, J.D. Baker and George C. Poston opened Baker, Poston & Company, the first chain of stores in Weatherford. At one time, the company's New York offices were on Broadway. Here, workers pose for a company photograph in 1923. On Thursday, March 6, 1930, Baker, Poston & Company, a leader in business for over 40 years, passed its business over to W.H. Bowden and Sons, which acquired the building and all the stock and furniture in the store. The company had announced three weeks earlier that it would be liquidating. (Courtesy of WPL.)

The McMahan grocery store, in business from 1912 to 1920, sold meats, produce, and other supplies. It was later moved to another location on the square. (Courtesy of WPL.)

The W.D. Taylor insurance firm dissolved its business as Taylor & Wythe, but on December 23, 1889, the business continued under the name Taylor & Taylor. The new firm adjusted all claims connected with the old firm, according to an article in the *Weekly Constitution* dated January 1, 1890. This photograph is from around 1900. (Courtesy of WPL.)

The Kuteman Block was built as a retail, office, and apartment building, as well as a café. On the site of the old Carson & Lewis Hotel, it was destroyed by fire on June 3, 1951. It is seen here in 1914. (Courtesy of WPL.)

The 4th Regiment minstrel parade was organized in September 1903 in the Sunday school room at Cumberland Presbyterian Church after a prayer meeting service. In May 1906, the band won first prize in a state contest for bands in Dallas. The band held several engagements in Dallas, Fort Worth, Cleburne, Mineral Wells, and other nearby cities. (Courtesy of WPL.)

This 1894 postcard shows shops on York Avenue, including a tin shop, a cobbler, a Chinese laundry, a carpenter, hardware stores, a wholesale grocery, the Carson & Lewis Hotel, and the Haynes Opera House. (Courtesy of WPL.)

W.D. Newberry Insurance was established in 1917 with a modern, air-conditioned, and well-equipped office. Newberry offered every type of insurance except life. At the time, the company was the largest insurance agency in the town. (Courtesy of WPL.)

Sturges & Company was founded on April 4, 1930, by Annie Sturges and James Churchhill Sturges. In May 1935, the store was moved to the Hopkins building, which burned in June 1935. After the fire, the business was temporarily run out of the dining room at the Hotel Parker. (Courtesy of WPL.)

This photograph of J.R. Lewis Hardware was taken after the remodel of the interior, which made the store quite organized. An advertisement placed in the local newspaper read, "First, Last and all the Time. We are ready to please our customers and friends, and in order to do so we have worked hard and long to secure such bargains as will please all." (Courtesy of WPL.)

K.S. Carter purchased J.R. Lewis Hardware and founded the Carter-Ivy Hardware Co., which operated on North Main Street beginning in 1904. Carter was only in partnership with Ivy for one year. (Trina Haynes.)

A customer of the Jim Pipkin tailor shop is getting fitted in this photograph, which would have served well as an advertisement for the business. (Courtesy of WPL.)

According to the *Weekly Herald* of November 18, 1948, the Montford Hotel was being rebuilt after a fire on October 18 in which one guest died. (Courtesy of WPL.)

This c. 1888 photograph of the square shows white stones in the left background in front of Rawlins Monuments. (Courtesy of V.A. Littleton.)

County attorney R.B. Hood (left) is seen in his office with his assistant Preston Martin in 1897. The two men eventually fought many legal battles against each other, but they remained friends. Martin was the father of Mary Martin, the mother of Larry Hagman. R.B. Hood began his legal practice in Weatherford in 1893, and was the county attorney for four years. (Courtesy of WPL.)

The former office of pharmacist Dr. W.B. Miller, the oldest brick building on the square, is now home to Weatherford Downtown Café. (Trina Haynes.)

The Blackwell House hotel was moved from this location to Fort Worth Highway in the late 1800s. An 1860 advertisement in the local newspaper read, "Blackwell house is now ready for accommodations of the traveling community and the public generally. The table will be furnished, at all times, with the best the country affords, and served up in good style. The proprietor, thankful for the past favors, hoped to receive a full share of patronage by his strict attention to business. J.W.H. Blackwell, Proprietor, September 13, 1860." (Trina Haynes.)

Cotton-Bratton Furniture Co. has been on the southeast corner of the square for over 100 years. The family business was started in 1883 at its present location by C.B. Rider. It was originally called the Rider-Yantis Company. When J.T. Cotton moved to Weatherford, he began working at the company, and later married Rider's daughter. In 1889, she and J.T. purchased the company from her mother. In 1911, the name was changed to the Cotton-Bratton Furniture Co. (Trina Haynes.)

The Franco Texas Land Co.'s building, constructed around 1880, is one of the oldest buildings on the square, built two years before the courthouse. The rooms upstairs were used by Gov. Samuel Lanham for his law office in 1896. The building is now owned by Bob Glenn, who has kept the door frame in Lanham's office intact to preserve the historical importance of the building. (Trina Haynes.)

The Knights of Pythias building had numerous tenants through the years, including John Leiper, who owned and operated the Leiper Music Store until his death in 1924. (Trina Haynes.)

Two

NORTHWEST TOUR

The oldest two-story home in Weatherford was built by R.W. Kindel. Starting in 1876, it took five years to complete. Kindel and his wife, Alison, raised eight children in the home. He was a pharmacist and an important founder of Weatherford. (Courtesy of WPL.)

The Weatherford, Mineral Wells & Northwestern Railway Company was chartered in 1889 and completed in 1891. The company owned two locomotives and 90 cars. In 1902, the line was bought by the Texas & Pacific Railway Company. In 1908, the railroad extended 18 miles from Mineral Wells to Graford. The new depot is seen here in the early 1900s. (Courtesy of WPL.)

The original Weatherford, Mineral Wells & Northwestern depot is seen here in the 1890s, just north of the tracks on North Main Street. (Courtesy of WPL.)

The Texas & Pacific depot is seen here on April 26, 1905. In April 1911, many visitors arrived at the depot for a dedication service for the newly built Knights of Pythias home on Bankhead Highway. (Courtesy of WPL.)

Greenwood Chapel was built in 1906, when parishioners came to church in horse-drawn buggies or on horseback. The church closed in 1967, and is now owned by the Greenwood Community Cemetery Association. It is now called Greenwood Memorial Chapel and is still used for special occasions. (Trina Haynes.)

The original Second Ward school building, not seen here, was a one-story, L-shaped frame structure. In 1900, it was replaced by the two-story, four-room rock structure below. As enrollment grew, more classrooms were added. In 1936, when the name was changed to William B. Travis Elementary School and a new, brick building was constructed, rock from this building was used to frame the entrance. (Both courtesy of WPL.)

The Parker County Roller Mills, built in 1892, was the third such plant in Texas. At that time, it only separated lint from the seed. The incorporators of the mill were R.H. Foat, F.C. Collier, W. White, and J.W. Corn. The mill operated for many years at full capacity; its three best years were 1900, 1906, and 1914. It was on North Main Street, just north of the Texas & Pacific Railroad tracks on the east side of the street. (Courtesy of WPL.)

This 1910 postcard of the Waldock home on Bridge Street shows Mrs. Waldock and her young daughter Margaret on the porch. (Courtesy of WPL.)

The rock Woodhouse home, built in 1909 as a country farmhouse, is now one of the largest in-town farms in Weatherford. The Woodhouse family purchased the farm around World War I, and then sold it in 1940. (Trina Haynes.)

The Diamond home, built in 1944, is seen here. Donald and Faye Diamond were very involved with politics, and held many meetings here with leaders of the Republican party, including Jim Wright. In the late 1940s, a second story was added, followed by many renovations over the years by different homeowners. (Trina Haynes.)

Three

Northeast Tour

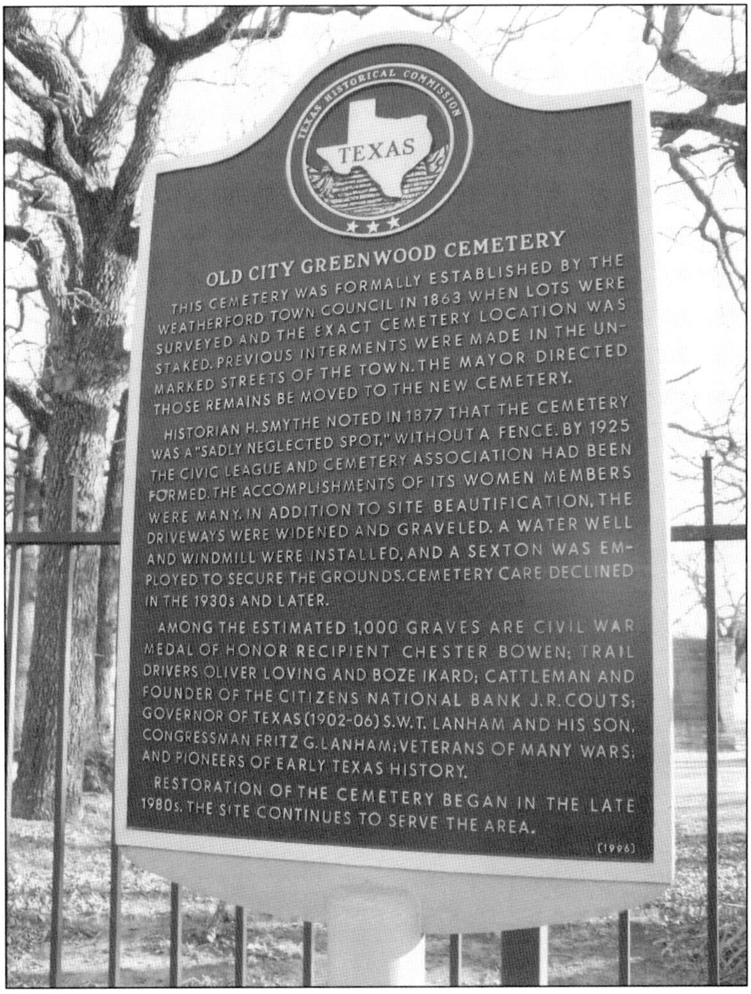

Greenwood Cemetery was established in 1863. Previous burials had been made in unmarked streets of the town, and the mayor had those moved to a new cemetery. In 1877, the cemetery was in poor shape and did not have a fence. A cemetery association was later formed, but care of the lot declined again in the 1930s. In the late 1980s, restoration of this historical cemetery began. (Trina Haynes.)

Baker Transfer Company started out as a horse-drawn carrier for deliveries. As time went on, it upgraded and owned the first local auto truck that hauled baggage, moved household goods, and moved freight locally and long-distance. There was a tower on top of the building with a bell that woke the locals in the morning. The stables were located on Dallas Avenue. (Courtesy of WPL.)

Captain Swain (1836–1883) and his wife and family are buried in Greenwood Cemetery in a vault known to some as the Witches Tomb. Captain Swain had a small flour mill on Front and North Main Streets. (Courtesy of WPL.)

Oliver Loving is buried in Greenwood Cemetery beside his wife, Susan, and some of his children. In 1858, Loving and a neighbor sent a herd of several hundred steers overland from Texas to Illinois. In 1860, he led the first herd out of Texas to the Colorado Territory. He did not return until after the Civil War, and he found that his family had moved to a home in Weatherford. (Trina Haynes.)

The home Loving's family moved to in Weatherford was located where the offices of the *Weatherford Democrat* are now, in order to be protected from Indians. Loving and his friend Charles Goodnight developed the Goodnight-Loving Trail. On September 25, 1867, Loving died from wounds suffered during an Indian attack. Goodnight took Loving's body back to Weatherford, where he was buried. (Trina Haynes.)

Bose Ikard had been born a slave and was brought to Weatherford when he was five years old. He was described as one of the best cowhands in the West. He worked alongside his friend Charles Goodnight and Oliver Loving. He is buried in Greenwood Cemetery. His stone reads: "1859–1928, served with me fours years on Goodnight-Loving Trail, never shirked a duty or disobeyed an order, rode with me on many stampedes with Commanches. Splendid Behavior-C Goodnight." (Trina Haynes.)

R.W. Kindel established the first castor oil mill in town on Front Street, just west of Greenwood Cemetery. Over the years, it was used by several entities, including the Carson & Lewis Hotel and the National Guard. Later, it was used by the Ku Klux Klan. The walls of the building, seen here, still stand, and the interior is used for storage of equipment. (Trina Haynes.)

Harry Waldock operated this butcher shop from 1891 to 1898. Bill Waldock is seen in this 1927 photograph of the interior of the shop, on North Main Street. (Courtesy of WPL.)

Bill Tanner is seen here around 1910 at left, on the white horse, at the livery stable behind where Albertson's is today. Tanner's son Leon and Mary Kemp grew up as close friends and keep their family ties together with ongoing friendship. (Courtesy of Leon Tanner.)

North Side Baptist Church was founded on June 14, 1897, and was originally called the Second Baptist Church. The first building was across the street from the current building, and the name was changed in 1908. This photograph was taken on June 1, 1925. (Courtesy of WPL.)

The tabernacle for North Side Baptist Church, seen here, was used for revivals and other gatherings. (Courtesy of WPL.)

The park at Sunshine Lake was given a new name, Cartwright Park, in honor of Grace Cartwright, who upon her retirement from the park board requested that the town creek that runs through the park be cleaned and given adequate lighting for hiking and bicycle trails. The bathhouse seen here no longer stands. (Courtesy of WPL.)

The 1908 old compress was located on Ft. Worth Street southeast of Santa Fe. The cotton compress industry developed in antebellum Texas because of the need to lower the cost of transporting cotton on sailing vessels. As cotton culture spread into the Texas hinterlands after the Civil War, compresses were built in many Texas towns in addition to the port cities. In the 1890s, processes were developed to compress cotton to a high density at gins, thus eliminating the need for cotton compresses. (Both courtesy of WPL.)

C.C. Baker was a successful business owner who ran the Baker Transfer Company. He started the business by offering transportation, at 25¢ per passenger, to and from all depots, hotels, and residences. (Courtesy of WPL.)

According to the July 22, 1943, *Weekly Herald*, Weatherford's public market, seen here, "is thriving in business with the sale of Parker county produce. A variety of produce is being sold at this time, including peaches, watermelons, cantaloupes, black eyed peas, okra, tomatoes, and grapes. A number of booths are in operation with large space being maintained by the Parker county fruit growers association. Individual farmers have booths of their own and others are operated by persons who buy their stock from farmers. A few trucks are being loaded daily with mixed cargoes of melons, cantaloupes, and vegetables. All produce is selling at war-time prices, the highest ever known here. In some cases the prices have dropped and sales are made much lower prices than earlier in the season." (Courtesy of WPL.)

The Weatherford post office was established on September 18, 1856. The first post office was on the square in a wooden building with dirt floors. After that, it moved to numerous locations. Its final move was on December 26, 1914, to where it still stands today on Fort Worth Street. It was built of brick in the classic Revival style at a cost of $60,000. (Trina Haynes.)

John and Addie Raper operated the Raper Hotel and boardinghouse (across the street) for many years on North Main Street. This photograph was taken in 1927 from Front Street, looking south down North Main Street. The building no longer stands. (Courtesy of WPL.)

The First Ward school is seen here in 1896. It was later named Bowie Elementary, but it is no longer a school. It now functions as a student-service building for faculty, and hosts activities for kids in the summer, such as sewing lessons. (Courtesy of WPL.)

The Galbreaith-Pickard Funeral Home, seen here, is in the original home of Elm Street Methodist Church, built in 1894. The church later changed its name to Couts Memorial Church in memory of J.R. Couts, the founder of Citizens National Bank. Galbreaith-Pickard has been in the building since 1945. (Trina Haynes.)

The Keaton home was built in 1910 in the late Victorian style by A.D. and Jennie Lee Keaton for $850. The original property had a smokehouse, a barn, a water/windmill tower, and a chicken house. It was the childhood home of R. Roy Keaton, who went on to become the director general of Lions Club International. (Trina Haynes.)

The Santa Fe Depot was completed in 1910. Due to Jim Crow laws, it had three separate waiting rooms, segregated by sex and color. This building is very well preserved and now houses the Weatherford Chamber of Commerce. (Trina Haynes.)

The King home, built before 1920, was one of two houses in the area built of native rock. Hollis Abner King operated a gravel pit on his land, which later became Parker County and Weatherford roadways. (Trina Haynes.)

The Brannan home was built in 1902 by Col. G.M. Bowie for his daughter Edith and her husband, James Brannan. This home contained many original features, including hardwood floors, copper doorknobs, a hand-carved staircase, and oak interior woodwork. The home no longer stands; in its place is the Parker County Agricultural Extension Agency. (Trina Haynes.)

Four

SOUTHEAST TOUR

On June 15, 1876, six students received their diplomas from Weatherford College. From 1889 to the early 1900s, Weatherford College changed hands many times, and went through many names trying to establish itself in the town. In the spring of 1969, the last remnants of Weatherford College were torn down and set on fire to clear the site. (Courtesy of WPL.)

Dr. David Switzer (center) and other faculty members pose for a photograph at Weatherford College. Dr. Switzer was the president of the college from 1875 until 1902, when he left to start his own college. (Courtesy of North Texas University Library.)

This 1953 postcard shows the Hotel Parker, which was considered one of the most modern hotels in the area and continued to operate into the 21st century. (Courtesy of WPL.)

In 1909, the Texas Pythian Home began as a home for widows and orphans. The main structure was used for orphan children, staff, and widows and their children. In 1914, a boys' dorm was built, and a girls' dorm was built in 1925. Widows no longer live at the Pythian home, but it is still an orphanage. The children attend Weatherford schools. (Both courtesy of WPL.)

Weatherford mayor G.A. Holland presented the city with a 234-acre park and lake. The park had a number of stone buildings, including the Wagoner-McCleskey log cabins, and the clear, spring-fed lake was a favorite swimming spot for residents. R.B. Hood was the speaker at the dedication of the Double Log Cabin (below) built at Holland Lake. (Both courtesy of WPL.)

The original wooden structure housing St. Stephens Catholic Church was built in 1882 and was destroyed by fire in 1902, when this redbrick church was built. It still has the original stained glass. In 1951, Douglas Chandor, of Chandor Gardens, helped with the beautification of the church and did not request pay. (Courtesy of WPL.)

This American La France pumper, seen here on April 15, 1955, at Weatherford fire station No. 3, was purchased brand new. In 1913, the fire department ordered the first American La France chemical truck, which it traded in for another truck in 1917 due to its inadequacies. The 1917 La France truck fought its last fire when the Kuteman Block burned in 1951. (Courtesy of WPL.)

First United Methodist Church was organized in 1857. For 10 years, it held services in the courthouse and in a schoolhouse, before a church was built in 1867. In 1886, a tornado destroyed the building, and services were held at the Masonic Institute, which later became Weatherford College. In 1888, construction on this building began. It was completed in 1891, and it still stands today. The interior of the church has gone through many renovations, but the exterior remains untouched. (Trina Haynes.)

The Doss Heritage and Cultural Center was once known as the Heritage Gallery and was located in the Weatherford Public Library. Thanks to volunteers from Civic Development Inc., it is now this 23,000-square-foot building that contains exhibits, including one displaying tapestries of cattle barons and cowboys, three galleries, and plenty of room for meetings, educational programs, small concerts, and many other events. (Trina Haynes.)

The MacKenzie home was built between 1900 and 1905 for Dr. John R. MacKenzie. After his death, his nephew Dr. William Y. MacKenzie purchased the home in 1912. In 1961, it was purchased by Weatherford College and used as a boys' dorm. It has since been restored back into a residence. (Trina Haynes.)

This home was constructed in 1898 by Parker County judge J.M. Richards. It was originally a one-story, three-room house, and has since undergone many renovations to make it a two-story, twelve-room home. In 1944, the home was used as a boardinghouse by a different owner, and it had four different kitchens for a time. (Trina Haynes.)

The land on this site was purchased in 1869, and changed hands many times until 1921, when it was purchased by Z.B. Mays. This bungalow-style home was built in 1922. In 2008, the cozy home was turned into the Rose Garden Cottage Bed & Breakfast. (Trina Haynes.)

The Smith home was built in 1879. Joshua Smith ran a prosperous mercantile business on the square. It was noted that he never turned anyone away because they could not pay. His wife, Carrie, served as the director of the Junior League for 17 years, as well as the Sunday school director, choir director, and organist for her church. She also provided a scholarship to educate nine Chinese girls. In 1964, Weatherford College purchased the home to use as the president's house, and later sold it to the Baptist Student Union. (Trina Haynes.)

One of the oldest car dealer in Weatherford, the Hobson Motor Company was established by W.L. Hobson more than 83 years ago. Business began at the present location on Fort Worth Street at South Elm; the original space only included what is now the firm's shops. Hobson has been a Dodge agent since opening. (Trina Haynes.)

Five

Southwest Tour

The new city hall, seen here, was built on the site of the first city hall, and was dedicated in early 1934. Bob Glenn's father, Clyde, was stationed there as a police officer and recalled that the old jail cell was still there and was still spooky. (Trina Haynes.)

One of the oldest businesses in Weatherford, Rawlins Monuments, was opened by Alex Rawlins in 1884. The monument shop is seen here around 1920. (Courtesy of V.A. Littleton.)

The C.D. Hartnett home was built in 1896. Hartnett, a wholesale grocer and banker, was the president of the First National Bank from 1894 to 1904 before returning to the grocery business. This house is now the Angel's Nest Bed & Breakfast. (Trina Haynes.)

The Howard Martin home was built before 1900. Martin was a prominent Weatherford attorney and the brother of fellow attorney Preston Martin. He was appointed Parker County attorney and won two reelections for the post. During Governor Lanham's first term, he appointed Howard Martin the assistant attorney general to represent the state before the court of criminal appeals. Howard was also a member of the Knights of Pythias, an organization that helped support the Pythian home for windows and orphans. (Trina Haynes.)

Seen here is the Justin Anderson home, built around 1900. Anderson was a minister and a professor at Weatherford College. Through the years, many renovations have taken place inside the home, but nothing has changed its exterior charm. (Trina Haynes.)

The Charles and James Barthold home was built in 1877 by Charles Barthold Sr. The brothers owned a very successful mercantile business. The home has stayed in the family, and members of the Barthold family are buried in Greenwood Cemetery. (Trina Haynes.)

The St. Clair home was built in 1985 as a reproduction of a saltbox-style house. Many homes from New England were purchased and dismantled, and parts of them were used to construct this home. Initially, the home had a rustic, dark wood character. It is now stained wood. (Trina Haynes.)

Edwin Barthold built this home in 1893. He was the brother of Charles and James Barthold. The home was originally two stories, and the porch wrapped around the side of the house. Also, the lot once extended out to Alamo Street. (Trina Haynes.)

Weatherford Middle School, now known as Shirley Hall Middle School, was built in 1967. It is Weatherford's oldest operating school building. (Trina Haynes.)

Weatherford Public Library is known for the quality of service it provides for the community, which includes a genealogy section and cabinets filled with local historical information. It is also the location of the Mary Martin statue, seen here. (Trina Haynes.)

Soldier Spring Park was a stopping point for soldiers, Indians, and visitors. A natural spring still flows there. An area within the park, formerly the Chautauqua grounds, is where the last legal hanging took place. The park once fell into disrepute, but it has since been kept up by the garden clubs. (Trina Haynes.)

The Samuel Willis Tucker Lanham home was built in 1871 and later enlarged. He and his wife lived there with their eight children. Lanham was the last Confederate governor of Texas. He and his wife both died in 1908, and are buried in Greenwood Cemetery. This photograph was taken on June 20, 1920. (Courtesy of WPL.)

Moses Sandburn Gordon purchased land in 1900 and built three houses on it in 1905. This was the first home he built—the other two were for his daughters. Later, one of the houses burned down; the other still stands just north of this home. (Trina Haynes.)

This electric and waterworks plant was located at the old Cherry Park. B.F. Cherry operated the plant; the city park is named in his honor. (Courtesy of WPL.)

The Campbell home was built in 1902. Dr. Campbell was a Weatherford physician who purchased the home around World War I and lived there until his death. Up until 2008, the local hospital was known as Campbell Memorial Hospital. This beautiful mansion sits upon a hill surrounded by wooded acres. (Trina Haynes.)

The Boyer home was built in 1886, and the second story was added in 1905. It was unchanged after that until a storm knocked over a chimney. Later, another chimney was constructed for the two fireplaces in the house. (Trina Haynes.)

The Edward Neer home is involved in an intriguing story. It was likely built in 1889 by Neer and his wife, Nellie. In 1890, a plat was filed with Parker County indicating that Neer owned all the properties along his street and on Davis Street. In that same year, all the county census records were destroyed in a suspicious fire before an upcoming murder trial. (Trina Haynes.)

R.J. Norton and his wife, Ida, completed this home in 1907. In 1901, Norton started the Weatherford Bottling Company and began making soft drinks, selling his company to Coca-Cola in 1918. Ida was a descendant of Robert Potter, who signed the Declaration of Independence and was the country's first secretary of the Navy. This home remains in the family today. (Trina Haynes.)

In 1890, the E.J. Neer home (also on the previous page) was a one-story house with three rooms. In 1900, Neer did his first renovation on the home, enlarging rooms and adding a kitchen, a bedroom, and porches. From 1945 to 1990, the home saw many changes to the floor plan. The current owners are trying to restore a better-organized floor plan. (Trina Haynes.)

The Jackly home was built in 1896, and a second story was added in 1906. The Victorian-style home is very well maintained, with Victorian ceilings and wooden moldings. (Trina Haynes.)

This sandstone building, constructed in 1904, is the South Main Church of Christ. The church, seen here in 1923, was formed after the Civil War, when 46 members of the Central Christian Church began to meet in a frame building on South Main Street. The Central Christian Church had begun in 1857, with members meeting on the West Fork of Sanchez Creek, just south of Weatherford. (Courtesy of WPL.)

The Zacharias-Barthold home was built in 1873 by cotton merchant Sigmund Zacharias. In 1887, Charles and Mattie Barthold bought the home, adding a second floor in 1900. From 1948 to 1973, the first floor was used to teach kindergarten. The original carriage house still stands behind the home. (Trina Haynes.)

In 1874, the Sullivan-Bell home was a two-room rock house. D.O. Sullivan was the postmaster of Weatherford. In 1894, the home was purchased by R.F. Bell, who enlarged it. The second story was added in 1905. (Trina Haynes.)

The Davis-Martin home was built in 1918 for Will Davis, a Weatherford banker. In 1924, the home was bought by Preston Martin, the father of Mary Martin, who was 11 years old at the time. This was her childhood home, as well as her son's, Larry Hagman. (Trina Haynes.)

Prince Memorial Church dates back to December 2, 1867. The church was named in honor of Rev. Bart Prince. A white minister, Rev. R.A. Elder, led the church in the beginning. The present church was built on the foundation of the original building in 1871. The first members were former slaves who wanted to have a church of their own. (Courtesy of WPL.)

The Potter home was built in 1895 and remodeled in 1915 by its new owners, but much of the exterior has remained the same, including the trim and the wraparound porch. (Trina Haynes.)

The Poston home was built in 1908 by George Poston, the owner of Baker, Poston & Company. In 1930, Art Deco light fixtures were added, along with oak floors. This home was the scene of many affairs, including the marriage of Poston's daughter, Mary. His business partner, J.D. Baker, had previously built a Victorian home across the street. (Trina Haynes.)

The Baker home was built in 1897 and completed in 1904 for the widow of J.D. Baker and her children. Baker had been the president of the Baker, Poston & Company, as well as the president of First National Bank for five years before his death in 1899. In 1908, Charles Baker, his son, took off on a trip and disappeared. Mrs. Baker posted signs, but nothing was ever discovered about her missing son. (Courtesy of WPL.)

J. Thomas Moore built this home in 1891. In 1950, a family room was added with a wood-burning fireplace. There are four other original wood-burning fireplaces in the home. (Trina Haynes.)

W.S. Fant, a Weatherford banker, built this home in 1890. Later, it was restored after being vacant for 25 years. In January 2008, a fire damaged the home. It was later bought and restored again. (Courtesy of WPL.)

The Eddleman-McFarland home was built in 1887 by banker W.H. Eddleman. Original features of the home included a three-story tower with a steep roof, servant's quarters, a barn, and corrals. The home was purchased by a dry goods merchant, Asa Grant, in December 1905. The Grant family removed the tower's third floor and steeple. In 1931, W.S. Fant purchased the home for his daughter Mrs. James Porter McFarland II. Their daughter, Louise McFarland, resided in the home until her death in 2007. (Trina Haynes.)

William E. Tate built this home in 1897. He was a Weatherford merchant who sold saddles, buggies, and hardware at his local business, Tate's Vehicle Repository. The restored Queen Anne–style mansion has 15 rooms, elaborate interior woodwork, five carved fireplace mantels, and a ballroom in which Larry Hagman attended a few dances. The Tate home was later turned into St. Botolph's Inn. Today, it is a private residence still owned by the caretakers of the inn. (Courtesy of WPL.)

The first school for African American students was built south of West Oak Street in 1917. A brick replacement structure, seen in both of these photographs, was built in 1927 and called Mt. Pleasant Colored School. It had two classrooms in which nine grades were taught. Until the 1960s, if African American students wanted to attend high school, they had to make their own arrangements. After many years of abandonment, a committee was formed to help restore and preserve this historic building. (Both Trina Haynes.)

The Sue Moore home was built in 1924 by her uncle Hank Shick. She bought it from him in December 1958 for "one dollar and love and affection." The home features a wraparound porch, original hardwood floors, a gas fireplace, original light fixtures, and an antique pedestal tub. (Trina Haynes.)

The Hemphill-Fant home was built by William Hemphill, part owner of Hemphill-Wells Dry Goods, and later purchased by First National Bank president W.S. Fant. The home includes original stained glass and a balcony. (Trina Haynes.)

The W.E. Richards home was built before 1907 by Walter E. Richards and his wife, Eva. Walter came to Weatherford in the 1890s. After moving here, he organized a football team and a baseball team. In 1899, he owned a sporting goods store on the southwest quadrant of the square, as well as the first Cadillac dealership and garage in Weatherford. In 1913, he was elected the first city councilman, and was a charter member of the Weatherford Chamber of Commerce. Walter and Eva were married in 1898. Her father was Rev. W.M. Bunch, a pioneer minister at Cumberland Presbyterian Church. (Trina Haynes.)

William Haas built this Queen Anne–style home in 1892. Haas owned a dry goods store on North Main Street. The home was built on what was known as Merchants Row, because of the great number of dry goods merchants who lived on the street. It was the first home in the city to have electricity, because it was located near Weatherford's first power plant, where Cherry Park now stands. (Trina Haynes.)

The Baker-Martin home was originally built by J.D. Baker in 1893. The property had stables and an orchard. Around 1900, Preston Martin, his wife, and their daughter Geraldine moved in. A second story was added in 1907. Famous Broadway star Mary Martin was born in the home in 1913. It is now Mama's Wish Bed & Breakfast. (Trina Haynes.)

The Milmo home was built in 1920. Members of the family lived there until their deaths. It was eventually sold to a new family, but the home has had only three families in its history. It sits on two lots near Cherry Park. (Trina Haynes.)

The Coker-White home was begun in 1892 and completed in 1902. The carriage house has three bays for horses and buggies, a tack room, and a servant's room on the second floor. The trees on the property are estimated to be 150 years old, and stand on what was once a town picnic area and campground. The house originally occupied the entire city block. At the time of construction, it was at the edge of the city limits. (Trina Haynes.)

This postcard shows the First Baptist Church in Weatherford, which was organized on July 5, 1856. It was originally called the United Missionary Baptist Church of Christ at Weatherford, and the name was shortened later. (Courtesy of WPL.)

Members of the All Saints Episcopal Church lay the cornerstone for a new building just south of city hall on April 18, 1923. The original church was located a block west of Church Street. Maggie Foat donated the property for the church. (Courtesy of WPL.)

The David S. Switzer home was built between 1890 and 1895 on the corner of Waco and Josephine Streets. Additions were made from 1899 to 1903 in order to board young ladies attending Weatherford College. Part of this historic home still stands on Waco Street. Switzer was the president of Weatherford College from 1875 until 1902 and was regarded as the father of the school. (Trina Haynes.)

The Jenkins home was built in 1917 by Clande and Mary Helm. O.S. and Eleanor Jenkins purchased it in 1926 and did some renovating, including enlarging the living room and moving the front entrance from Couts Street to Waco Street. The Jenkinses owned a dry goods store on the northwest corner of the square. (Trina Haynes.)

The Kuteman Hill home was built in 1918 as a one-and-a-half-story airplane bungalow. The home belonged to Elmer and Ina Kuteman Hill. Ina later divorced Elmer and married British portraitist Douglas Chandor, and together they created White Shadows Gardens, later called Chandor Gardens. (Trina Haynes.)

William and Francis Chew built this home in 1904 and lived there until 1943. William owned the Weatherford lumberyard for many years. (Trina Haynes.)

The Milliken home was built as a single-story house in 1883. In either 1903 or 1907, a second story was added. Robert Bruce Milliken was the postmaster of Weatherford. The home seen here was torn down and replaced with another on the same spot, and parts from the original home were used to make the current one. (Trina Haynes.)

Emmet and Ella Hatcher built this home in 1901. Emmet and his father were dry goods merchants and owned a business on North Main Street that offered the city's first delivery service. After Emmet's death in 1910, the home changed owners and eventually fell into disrepair in the 1970s. It was condemned and slated for demolition, but was salvaged at the last minute and restored. In February 1987, the home received the Weatherford Community Revitalization Property of the Month Award. (Trina Haynes.)

The Hood home was originally a one-story farmhouse in the 1800s. Prominent attorney R.B. Hood bought it in 1909 and added a second story. The home's original windmill still stands today and provides landscaping irrigation. (Trina Haynes.)

The Bradford home was built in 1920. Described as a Prairie-style bungalow, it features a roomy covered porch with substantial square columns and its original windows. In 1950, a master bedroom was added. (Trina Haynes.)

Maj. B.G. Bidwell, a Civil War veteran, built this home in 1889. It was first located on Oak Street, but moved to its current site on South Waco Street when it was remodeled in 1916. (Trina Haynes.)

The Third Ward school was located on Josephine and Lee Streets. Except for the Third Ward, the original wards were eventually renamed: the First Ward as Bowie Elementary, the Second Ward as Travis Elementary, the Fourth Ward as T.W. Stanley Elementary, and the Fifth Ward as Crocket Elementary. (Courtesy of V.A. Littleton.)

Isaac N. and Annie (Loving) Roach built this cottage in 1891. Roach fought in the Civil War and was an attorney, legislator, county judge, and president of the board of trustees of the Texas Female Seminary. Annie Loving Roach was the daughter of Oliver Loving. The Loving home, as it has come to be known, turned 120 in 2011. (Trina Haynes.)

C.W. Putnam built this home in the early 1900s. He purchased the land in 1892 from Cumberland Presbyterian Church. Putnam owned a jewelry store in the old Shropshire drugstore on the square. The home is now the Gingerbread House Bed & Breakfast. (Trina Haynes.)

The Tandy home was built between 1889 and 1900 for G.A. Tandy and his wife, Frankie Hutchison Tandy, by her brother, John Y. Hutchinson. The Tandys' daughter, Annie Hutchison Tandy, married Alexander Rawlins, the founder of Rawlins Monuments. In 1901, tragedy struck the Tandy family when two of their sons and their wives died from illness and an accident within a few weeks of each other. Mrs. Tandy was left to raise four orphaned grandchildren in this house. She lived here until her death, on December 3, 1926. (Trina Haynes.)

J.R. Williams, a carpenter and cabinetmaker, built this home in 1891. He sold the home to W.R. Freear, who owned a furniture store and a funeral home on North Main Street. Freear enlarged the home by adding a second story in 1902, and lived there until 1912. (Trina Haynes.)

J.R. Lewis built this Queen Anne–style home in 1899 for his wife and 10 children. He moved to Weatherford in 1844 and opened a tinning business. Lewis went on to become a city councilman, a wealthy businessman, and an elder at Grace Presbyterian Church. The historic house is now the home of Providence Title Company. (Both courtesy of WPL.)

Texas Female Seminary was sponsored by Cumberland Presbyterian Church and later renamed Texas Fairemont College. The school was in operation from 1889 to 1911, and officially closed in 1916. It continued to be used as a sanatorium and a nurses' school until 1929. Today, Emmanuel Baptist Church is on the site of the old seminary. (Below, courtesy of WPL.)

The J.T. Cotton home was built in 1896 on Oak Street. In 1889, Cotton established a furniture company and the Cotton-Bratton Funeral Home. (Courtesy of WPL.)

The old Lowe-Carter Hardware building also held the business of E.A. Frantz machinery. Frantz had numerous invention credits, including a buckle and machinery for baling cotton. He also had a factory out of state. One of his employees patented an improvement for the buckle. (Trina Haynes.)

Six

Far and Away

This photograph was taken on Sunday, May 15, 1988, at the dedication of the Texas historical marker for the Parker County Poor Farm and Cemetery. Pictured are representatives of the Parker County Historical Commission and the Abandoned Cemetery Association. The association helped with the cleanup, documentation of burials, and maintenance of this historic site. (Courtesy of Mary Kemp.)

The Parker County Poor Farm was created in 1883 and operated until 1946. It housed the county's elderly and poor citizens, and some convicts were sent there to work off fines by raising livestock and growing crops. Residents of the poor farm are seen here sitting on the porch around 1930. (Courtesy of WPL.)

The caretaker's home and a barn are seen here in 1986. The cemetery, located south of the caretaker's home, is where most of the residents were buried. Within one 15-year period, the poor farm had 15 different superintendents. (Courtesy of Mary Kemp.)

On a coon-hunting trip in the 1950s, V. Kemp Jr. accidentally found this cemetery. Years later, he and his wife, Mary Kemp, and some friends helped commission the restoration of the farm and cemetery as a historic site. Oatis Haynes told a similar story about wandering about and tripping over a rock, which he realized was a headstone. A total of 40 graves have been located in the cemetery, one of which belonged to a child, and only one of which had a headstone. (Both courtesy of Mary Kemp.)

There are 34 unknown burials at the Parker County Poor Farm Cemetery. Mary Kemp and Billie Bell researched the records at the Cotton-Bratton Funeral Home and discovered the names of 12 to 15 other people buried elsewhere. V. Kemp Jr. and Lowell Sullivan Jr. marked the graves with bricks until stones were put in place. A fence was placed around the cemetery, which now sits on private land. The tall marker below is inscribed with the names of those who died at the poor farm but are buried at other locations around Parker County. (Both courtesy of Mary Kemp.)

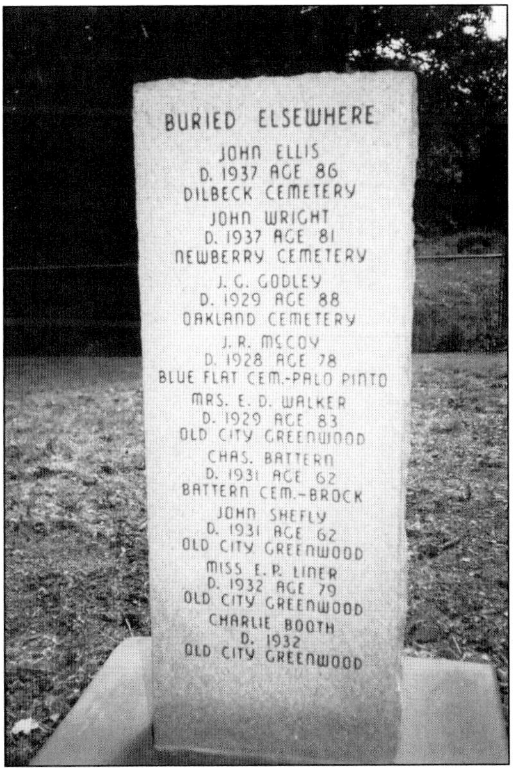

On April 8, 1905, county commissioners rode by buggy to the southern part of the county to inspect sites suggested for bridges to cross the river. They selected locations in what was known as Hightower Valley (now known as the Tin Top community), and at Brannon's Crossing, a few miles upstream. A pair of almost identical suspension bridges were built across the Brazos River in the two locations. Brannon's Bridge (above) was completed in January 1906. It was a very impressive structure at the time. (Courtesy of WPL.)

In 1855, Parker County was created and named after state representative Isaac Parker, who is buried in Turner Cemetery on Ragle Road northeast of Lake Weatherford. Parker's first family is buried in Hurst and his second family is buried here. His home place was south of the graveyard. (Courtesy of WPL.)

On Tuesday afternoon, February 14, 1956, Congressman Jim Wright gave the address at the ground-breaking ceremony at the site of the dam for Lake Weatherford. He said, "Here on this site, a dam will soon stretch across the valley for almost a mile. Where it will stream, it will rise 53 feet in the air. As the rains fall on the slopes of the Clear Fork basin, a lake of water will begin to collect here at the foot of the dam, and eventually 20,000 acre-feet of water will reach upward to the edges of a 13 mile water line." It was a historic day for Weatherford, as the dam meant water that could power machines, lawns, and laundry. (Trina Haynes.)